Blockchain:

Real-World Applications
And Understanding

How Blockchain Can Be Applied In Your World

WAYNE WALKER

TABLE OF CONTENTS

WHAT IS BLOCKCHAIN?

I n 2008 the first blockchain was designed by Satoshi Nakamoto who introduced the idea in a white paper with Bitcoin. Bitcoin was the first execution of the technology. Blockchain is a *type* of Distributed Ledger Technology (DLT). A distributed ledger is replicated, shared, and synchronized data geographically spread across sites, institutions, or countries. It is important to note from the beginning that *Distributed ledgers do not have a central administrator.* DLT is the underlying technology for Bitcoin and other cryptocurrencies.

A Different Tool for Different People

Cryptocurrencies are of least importance to a blockchain specialist because it does a lot more! As a matter of fact some blockchainers, as I like to call them, sometimes get annoyed when you bring up the topic of cryptocurrencies at their events.

For crypto enthusiasts, blockchain is the technical backbone of digital currencies. The developers use it for storing data on a distributed network and for the futurists it is a tool for creating a decentralized society.

Blockchain Building Blocks

Every block in a ledger is connected to the previous block by a cryptographic algorithm called a hash. The linked blocks form a chain, thus giving us the term "blockchain."

Blockchain is a form of database that is distributed, and operates on a consensus basis. The computers on the network, known as nodes, validate transactions and adds them to the blockchain. With no centralized source to verify changes, a distributed consensus algorithm is used to create agreement between nodes so that the same entry is made to each ledger.

Decentralization: Each party on a blockchain has access to the entire database and its complete history. Every party can validate the records of its partners without an intermediary.

Immutability: Each block has a timestamp and link to the previous block. The blocks are resistant to modifications. Once recorded, the data in any block cannot be altered retroactively without the alteration of all subsequent blocks. Algorithms are deployed to ensure the recording in the database is permanent.

Peer-2-Peer (P2P) Transmission: Communication occurs directly between peers without a central node.

Programmable: The transactions can be programmed. Users can set up algorithms and rules that automatically trigger transactions between nodes.

Let's Get Nerdy

A block contains data, its hash, and the hash of the previous block. Now let us get a little deeper in the explanation:

Data: The data stored depends on the type of block. For example with a cryptocurrency it might contain information on the sender, receiver, and the amount of the transaction.

Its hash: Once a block is created the hash is calculated. The hash is unique, basically it is the fingerprint for the block. It identifies both the block and its contents.

Hash: Hash of the previous block.

An example: Block 4 has its own hash, plus the hash of block 3. Only block 1 has no previous hash and this is known as the Genesis Block. If you alter the hash of block 3, all subsequent blocks are invalid because block 4 already has the correct hash of the previous block (block 3). Therefore all other bocks after 3 are invalid.

The distributed P2P network: If you alter the hash of block 3 when sent to the network it will be rejected by the other nodes (because it was altered).

To succeed with tampering, you must alter all the blocks. Redo the Proof-of-Work of each block to take control of 51% of the P2P network. *Proof-of-Work: Slows down the creation of new blocks.

Proof-of-Work: Is the most used method of establishing consensus. Proof-of-Work consensus requires each node to solve an extremely complex equation in order to complete each block. The point of the complexity of the equation is to force each node to use a significant amount of processing power and electricity in order to solve it. An expanded definition is provided in the "Blockchain First Aid" chapter later on in the book.

Types of Blockchains

The first is a permissionless or public blockchain, which means that anyone can access it. Next is a permissioned which is private. This is a closed network of nodes and only those relevant to the transactions can gain access. This is best for governments, hospitals, insurers, etc. There is also a hybrid blockchain where anyone can access it but not all can make updates. Another hybrid version could be some data is readable to the public, some of it is not.

Keep in Mind

Blockchain really shines best in low-trust environments. These are situations where participants are unable to deal directly with each other or lack a trusted intermediary.

Blockchain verifies but does NOT validate therefore, garbage in garbage out. False data could have been entered, this also applies to all off-chain data. It is only as strong as the weakest link, for example if sensors registering data are incorrect the blockchain is incorrect.

People also need to remember that lot of the technology involved is first world so it is not for everyone and it cannot solve all problems. The technology and human systems must be aligned.

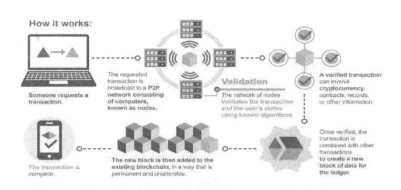

Figure 2: Blockchain and key features at a glance

A Basic Blockhain Network

DO YOU NEED BLOCKHAIN?

I n my effort to reduce some of the unneeded hype around blockchain technology we will review the questions that must be answered before setting up a network.

Is the database being considered likely to be attacked or do you need redundant copies on multiple distributed computers? If yes, then there is possible need for a blockchain. If no, then there is no need for a blockchain.

Does more than one participant need to update the data? If yes, then possible need for a blockchain. However if they trust each other, then no. If they would trust a third party, also no.

Does the data need to be kept private? Yes, then a need for blockchain.

Do you need to control who can make changes to the blockchain? If yes, you might need a permissioned blockchain.

A no answer to the previous two questions leads to a possible need of a public blockchain.

Before Getting on the Blockchain Train

Before launching a blockchain project, you should investigate if your or some traditional database technology can meet your needs. It is essential to clarify if the problem requires blockchain technology instead of going blockchain and then attempting to see if you have any use for it.

Any business case for blockchain must also account for the potential costs beyond hosting, licensing, and implementation. Much of the dramatic cost saving predictions, especially in the finance sector with replacing legacy systems is unlikely at the levels predicted. The hype often fails to sufficiently account for future costs in power and storage. Energy expenses may increase significantly as transactions volume goes up. The increased storage costs are because each node must maintain a ledger of all transactions from the beginning of the blockchain. Along with the technical aspects, employee education on blockchain and the practical adaptations must be included in the strategy.

INVESTMENT IN BLOCKCHAIN BY SECTORS

Blockchain remains a relatively young technology. Most of the short- term value will be in cost reduction. The hospitality, automotive, and financial services are some of the early adopters. In the financial services alone, so far 90 plus major banks in the United States, Canada and Europe are *already* testing blockchain solutions.

Some of the biggest finance names like Citi and Bank of America are busy securing patents to capture certain segments of the market. The segments include wire transfers, payment systems, and even their own cryptocurrencies.

Practical Applications and Real World Use

- New York Interactive Advertising Exchange (NYIAX): Is using blockchain as a way to provide an ads marketplace for publishers.

- Maersk: Has blockchain based projects for maritime logistics to explore potential cost savings. This is due to the expense of verifying freight documents which is sometimes more costly than the shipping. This expensive process involves over 200 persons that includes agents, government officials, and agencies.

- DeBeers: Uses the technology to track the import and sale of diamonds.

- Essentia: Uses blockchain to store passenger data in the Netherlands.

Not So Virgin

Food safety and traceability is an important topic for all countries. There is the from "farm to fork" process where food is tracked from production-> to distribution-> to retailers. For example, with blockchain technology if something is contaminated you can now destroy specific batches and not everything, which has been the normal practice.

The technology can also be unleashed to reduce fake and altered food products. The story that grabbed my attention the most was that in Europe there is more extra virgin olive oil in supply than what is actually produced. How is this possible? Because fake extra virgin olive oil is as profitable as dealing illegal narcotics, but without the risk. In a 2015 Danish food safety team random check of a 35 bottle case labelled extra virgin, only 6 were extra virgin, 12 were so bad they could not be sold to the public. One of several possible explanations, is that it all began with the distributor who certified that a supplier is "trusted." The supplier will normally provide the first few shipments as agreed, and then to increase profits they begin to slip in fakes with the future shipments.

This is not unique to Denmark or olive oil, unfortunately it happens in other countries and with other products. When I read about this case and researched further I was stunned to find out that much of the extra virgin olive oil on the market is neither extra virgin or from the country that is on the bottle label. For those that want to dive in deeper there are plenty of stories and sources on the web to follow up on.

Blockchain and Real Estate

The real estate industry is also one of the areas getting a lot of attention from blockchain specialists. Buying a home is considered a rite of passage into adulthood for many people across the globe and blockchain offers a new way to accomplish this. You can use the technology to transfer property to another party in a process that is secure, legitimate, and safe.

The current real estate market struggles with the problems of fake listings, document forgery and rental scams. The home selling process is cumbersome and is not exactly known for its speed. With smart contracts, documents and contracts are connected to a blockchain. These records are immutable, permanent and transparent. This will include an accounting system where transactions are automatically recorded and balanced without the fear of manipulation. Each individual or corporation will have a secure electronic record showing all the details. This will help to ensure that property fraud and paper deeds become things of the past.

Mini Case Study

In my research for the book, I came across a firm in the New York City area that has an innovative platform designed to service the financial sector. The platform serves as a marketplace for banks to display and sell their properties directly to homebuyers and developers. Properties are digitally sold, all initiated by smart contracts and recorded onto a private blockchain.

The platform showcases preset documents and contracts for e- signature, that minimizing the back-and-forth follow-up, and simplifies the signing process for banks and home buyers. All documents are recorded and tracked on the blockchain. Users are able to browse profiles and connect with real estate brokers, agents, lawyers, inspectors, and other professionals directly.

Similar to some famous payment systems like PayPal the platform processes online payments and transactions. The payments for real estate services and property purchases are powered by smart contracts, then recorded and tracked on their blockchain.

The users are also able to view up-to-date floor plans, property photos, 3D walk-throughs, digital videos and drone shots of the properties. They also receive a secure online wallet. They can store, receive or send digital payments to other users on the platform and yes, all payments are recorded and tracked on their private blockchain.

Obviously this is not the only firm in this sector. From my research and what anyone can confirm with a simple search on the web is that there are many firms exploring opportunities in the blockchain real estate space. I predict that of all the industries seeking practical applications of blockchain technology real estate will be one of the easiest matches.

BLOCKCHAIN AS A SERVICE (BAAS)

BaaS provides companies the opportunity to test blockchain technology without the full financial or organizational risk of developing it themselves. Organizations can evaluate the technology for their specific needs *before* adoption. Microsoft's Azure and IBM's Hyperledger are two of the best-known BaaS examples.

Developers are also busy generating their own decentralized apps on platforms such as Ethereum. Others are using the platforms to generate escrow smart contracts. These different platform options also gives developer teams opportunities to create and use their own tokens that allows them to hold ICOs.

Build Your Own Blockchain?

Ethereum allows you to create your own test blockchain network, a demo version. It is identical to the main Ethereum chain, except that transactions and smart contracts on this network are only accessible to nodes that are connected to it.

To become a node in the Ethereum network, your computer needs to download and update a copy of the entire Ethereum blockchain. They also provide the tools to download in order to interact with the network. These are, Eth and Geth.

After setting up a test blockchain, you can build smart contracts, make transactions and even distributed apps without needing real Ether. To get started, you create some fake Ether, add it to your account and then use it to make transactions.

SMART CONTRACTS

A smart contract is a digitally enforceable contract and computer program that is stored inside of a blockchain. This is the next generation or as some describe it, the evolution of blockchains. It transforms the blockchain from a system of distributed ledgers into a new way to store, transfer, and communicate between the parts of a network.

The terms of the agreement or operation are written into lines of code which are executed when triggered by certain events. The contracts can be used to automate basic operations on a network, thus removing the need for a trusted third party.

A smart contract might allow you to send Ether on a certain date, similar to a direct payment, except that it is automated and transparent. The user creates a contract and thereafter add sufficient Ether to execute the command. Each transaction made through the contract is then recorded and updated on the blockchain.

A note: Ether is the native currency to the Ethereum blockchain.

Platform and Language

Ethereum was created and designed to support smart contracts. The Ethereum Virtual Machine (EVM) runs the contracts. This is a part of the Ethereum platform which consist of EVM, plus the Ethereum blockchain.

Solidity is the programming language used. It shares some rules and principles (syntax) of JavaScript. Ethereum has been fortunate to attract a broad community of developers and enterprises that have developed the capacity of the network by building decentralized applications.

Smart Contracts: Legally Enforceable?

Currently they are not legally enforceable, code is not law, but that might change in the future. As we know, people generally think of contracts as agreements that can be legally enforced. Smart contracts were not intended to be legally enforced. You also cannot make an illegal contract. For example a contract to commit an illegal act is not valid or enforceable.

Keep in mind, contracts require counterparties, smart contracts do not. When things do not go as planned, who do you sue? The network? The network miners? The person or team who wrote the code? Identifying a wallet address on a blockchain is not the easiest task to accomplish. A smart contract has no guarantee that you will be able to find out who used your agreement. A lawsuit must be filed against an individual. If you do not know who the other party is, then there is no case. You cannot take "no one" to court.

What happens when mistakes are in the code, leaving it open to malicious use or if transactions need to be altered or reversed? Smart contracts do not deal with ambiguity or uncertainty, which leads some cynics to complain "then they are not so smart." The reality is that programmers cannot be asked to plan for every contingency. The immutable method of enforcement also ensures that once all parties have entered a smart contract it will be carried out regardless of any other factor.

Smart Contracts: DAO

Distributed Autonomous Organization (DAO): A real-world mess. The largest smart contract to date, an investment vehicle that enabled members to participate by using their private cryptographic keys to vote on what the fund should invest in. No lawyers, no management fees. They boasted DAO "removes the ability of directors and fund managers to waste investor funds."

Due to a software bug, the DAO voted to invest $50 million of members' money into a vehicle controlled by programmers who discovered weaknesses in the software. Some said it was a hack because the software did not function as planned, others disagreed, stating that the software made decisions autonomously and if you did not understand how it worked you should not have joined.

Members watched the attackers drain the funds and they were powerless to stop it. In the end, people voted to amend the software contract and Ethereum's lead coders reversed the transaction history and returned the money to its original owners.

SMART CONTRACTS: THE "UNDO" RULE

Ho w can we get relief after a mistake? Smart laws introduce human logic to the situation. This is a combination of current law mixed with distributed ledger technology so that justice can be done. A network can have a "undo" rule so that when executed, it is able to transfer any digital asset from one account to another. A scenario could include, that the law has a section where one member is selected and given the authority to launch the special "undo" law that freezes funds. This can be done with an algorithm. This should, in theory, reduce the incentive to steal assets since they can later be frozen and returned to the victim's account.

Another issue for members to consider is that the executor could make an error when executing the decision to freeze an account. The network then has to decide when compared to the consequences of inaction, if an error leading to the accidental stop of a contract might be the acceptable lesser of two evils.

WHAT IS AN ICO?

According to a recent survey, the majority of American adults did not know what an ICO was and given the current environment that is understandable. In this chapter we will clear things up.

An Initial Coin Offering (ICO) is similar to an Initial Public Offering (IPO). In IPOs investors are asked to purchase shares of a company in the company's attempt to raise capital. However, with ICOs, investors purchase the underlying crypto tokens and they make the payment using either Bitcoin or Ether.

The first ICO was the MasterCoin Project in 2013 by J R Willet. It raised $500,000 in the form of 5,000 Bitcoins. Investors purchased MasterCoins in exchange for Bitcoins. The 5,000 Bitcoins that MasterCoin raised in 2013 was worth about $41 million in June 2018.

ICOs are popular and for now it appears that regulators remain a step behind in the action. In an attempt to catch up, several countries have placed limitations on their citizens' ability to participate. This protects people from some ICO scams but it also prevents them from getting involved in potentially profitable opportunities.

Currently, the easy money days are gone. Having just a white paper with no financial statements or evidence that the company exists and expecting that funds will roll in is a thing of the past. From 2018 on, it is more difficult to raise money, but if the project is good you are rewarded more. More funds, $9 billion was raised in the first 4 months of 2018 than all of 2017 with $6.1 billion.

USA Special Rules

Raising money through ICOs in the United States comes with some regulations specific to the US. One is Reg D 506(c), it is relatively easy and quick to comply with. There is no cap on the amount that you can raise; you file a form D. The downside is that you are limited to raising money from accredited investors. An accredited investor is a person that earns at least $200,000 per year or has at least a million US Dollars in assets outside of their primary residence.

The other regulation is Reg A, you can raise up to $50 million, you can solicit or market the deal, and anyone over 18 globally can invest. It is costly and time-consuming and it also requires filing with the SEC, plus 2 years of audited financials.

Both of these regulations have led to some projects bypassing the United States in favor of other countries with more relaxed rules.

Comparing ICOs with Traditional Funding

ICOs globally are mostly unregulated. In the US, the Securities and Exchange Commission (SEC) has reacted and considers many of them as securities. ICOs pass the Howey test and this means that security regulations apply.

In traditional funding, you pay to own a percentage of a company. The percentage owned is constant and so is the dollar amount that you paid. To launch an IPO, a company needs to satisfy a list of requirements that includes earnings threshold, verification of accounts, minimum market capitalization, etc.

In the world of ICOs the owners can raise funds without cumbersome shareholder agreements. When they get Bitcoin or Ether, the company does not give up equity in exchange for the investment that was made. You only invest in the development of a firm's technology or project but not in the firm. To be very clear, you have no ownership stake in the firm itself.

The dollar value of the Bitcoin or Ether received in the exchange can increase and obviously it can also go down. For example, an ICO raises $5 million of Bitcoins in September, the amount raised can be worth $8 million in December.

TOKEN EVOLUTION

A token is launched through an ICO. They are issued to investors in exchange for either Bitcoin or Ether. After the ICO, the public can buy, sell, or hold the tokens in the same way they can with a stock. Investors hope that the tokens will increase in enough value that they will be able to cash out with a profit.

Ethereum technology provides the base on which tokens are built. It is the market leader for tokens (for now). There are currently over 70,000 tokens on the Ethereum network. For the adventurous ones there are several sites that even allow you to create your own.

Tokens can represent anything from real commodities to currencies used in blockchain ecosystems. Bottom line, a coin does one thing and programmable tokens can fulfil many types of functions.

ERC20

ERC20 (Ethereum Request for Comment), is the guideline followed when creating tokens. It standardizes token smart contracts by eliminating the need for exchanges and wallets to create a custom code for each token. ERC20 tokens are used by most ICOs.

Currency Tokens

The original currency token is Bitcoin and it is still the leader. Currency tokens are designed to be digital cash: They are used in the exchange of goods and services or traded on the market. They are not legal tender as yet but let us see how their stories unfold. Their values are based mostly on speculation and the usual conditions of supply and demand.

Utility Tokens

Ethereum was the first major utility token and it also does duty as a currency token. Utility tokens allows you to do things. This, for example, can take the form of running smart contracts on the blockchain. Utility tokens are sometimes referred to as Network Access Tokens. They give you access to something a network offers.

Asset Tokens

They represent some sort of asset or product. The tokens can also represent ownership or the right of use. There is the risk that if the underlying asset depreciates, so does the token. The obvious goal is to tokenize things that are expected to increase in value and it could even include traditional assets like gold.

Equity Tokens

Like a stock, an equity token buys a degree of ownership of an organization. An equity token implies ownership and control. The Ethereum based DAO was the first major equity token. Owners of DAO tokens had control over the activities of the organization.

The rules of what is an equity can be unclear depending on whom you speak to. I suggest that you consult a lawyer. If the token provides you a reward or benefit off the actions of others, or if the token involves making money exclusively off the actions of others, it might be an equity (this brings regulations).

Reputation and Reward Tokens

These are given as symbols of reputation or rewards. They are a way of specifying on a blockchain that some user or wallet did something special or is someone special.

The value of a reputation token is that you can trust that the person in possession of one is who they say they are.

Security Token Offerings?

Security Token Offerings (STOs) are regulated offerings in which the issuer sells programmable equity to investors. STOs come with additional complexity that includes lots of paperwork, lawyers, underwriting, and regulations. STOs are often seen as more stable and legitimate than some ICOs, as they can provide investors upfront reassurance that they are less likely to run into problems later.

The Latest in Token Evolution (FYI)

ERC721: Has been adopted as the standard token for deploying digital art or unique collectibles on the blockchain and blockchain gaming apps.

ERC1155: The latest token entering the blockchain gaming world. Both are non-fungible, each token is unique.

Token Evolution (ERC20 FYI)

This is a little extra for those that want to know the guidelines that must be followed for ERC20 tokens creation.

Total Supply: defines the total supply of tokens. When this limit is reached the smart contract stops issuing more tokens.

Balance of: indicates how many tokens a given address has.

Transfer: takes a certain amount of tokens from the total supply and gives to a user.

Transfer From: can be used to transfer tokens between any two users that have them.

Approve: verifies that your contract can give a certain amount of tokens to a user.

Allowance: checks if a user has enough balance to send a certain amount to tokens to another user.

ICO RATINGS, CAN YOU TRUST THEM?

Ratings are important because inexperienced investors are especially trusting of ICO rating platforms when seeking information before investing. The reality is that rating platforms have always been looked at with suspicion among more experienced market players. To begin, it is relatively easy to buy ICO ratings, therefore ratings on ICO sites in many, many cases are not independent.

"ICO ratings from a trusted source" is a version of what ICO rating platforms advertise on their websites to gain the trust of investors looking for information. A nice claim, but investigations of the websites showed that an ICO rating's visibility is not always impartial. The results are frightening, the players basically "pay to play."

Many platforms are nothing more than marketing sites selling to the highest bidders. They offer prime listing services in exchange for payment. ICOs can secure a top tier ranking in an ICO overview and be featured in special mailings. If the ICO is willing to pay up, the site can block their competitors from appearing on the profile pages of the paying ICO. These paid top listings are not labelled as sponsored.

If you already have a rating that is not that high, it is not unheard of to be contacted by services offering to boost it.

Keep in mind inexperienced investors use this information to make investment decisions which is a serious problem.

WHAT IS NEXT FOR BLOCKCHAINS?

Directed Acyclic Graphs (DAGs)

D irected Acyclic Graphs are not completely new, in 2015 the first proposal was introduced to mix it with blockchain technology. Sergio Lerner introduced the idea with a project that he was working on, the project failed, but it opened the door for developers to expand upon the DAG concept. DAGs are not blockchains, there is no chain which links all the blocks. There are no blocks at all and the transactions on individual nodes do not need to be synchronized with any other. This allows transactions to occur without the confirmation of the entire network, significantly reducing the normal confirmation time.

How do DAGs Work?

On a DAG there is no need for miner rewards and there are no transaction fees for the end user. Transactions are confirmed through a process where a user confirms two previous transactions in order for their own transactions to be processed.

Every transaction acts as its own block, and these can be stored in different locations, on multiple devices, before syncing up with a node somewhere on the graph. The syncing process updates the ledger with the final transaction details of all the interactions that took place among the addresses on the graph.

IOTA is probably the most well-known adopter of DAG technology. They refer to it as the Tangle. Tangle is the web that makes up IOTA's network of users who serve as both transactors and verifiers at the same time. To issue a transaction, users must work to approve other transactions. The assumption is the nodes will insure that the approved transactions are not conflicting and will not approve those that do. As a transaction gets more approvals, it becomes more accepted by the system.

All technology comes with its weak points. DAG coins claim to be quantum-resistant, but there is uncertainty about their ability to survive a 33% attack. This is the amount of computing power necessary to attack and take over a Proof-of-Stake DAG network.

There are also concerns over the ability for DAG networks to be fully decentralized. Since validations by all nodes on the network is not required, there are more opportunities for misconduct, the main one being double spend. To protect against this scenario, many DAG projects have coordinator nodes. This brings a centralized element and ensures a linear order of transactions within the DAG. The

IOTA developers run their own coordinator node at all times in order to protect the network.

The concerns of centralization that exist with DAGs also exist with Bitcoin and other cryptos that can be heavily influenced by a small number of large traders known as whales.

BLOCKCHAIN FIRST AID KIT

This chapter has the blockchain "first aid" kit. These are the terms and concepts that I believe are essential to know in addition to the content from the previous chapters. The "kit" has the terms conveniently compiled by sections for you. Study them and you will noticeably improve your understanding of blockchain technology.

Double-spending: a potential flaw in cryptos is the risk that a digital currency can be spent twice. This is possible because a token consists of a digital file that can be duplicated or falsified. Cryptographic techniques are used to prevent double-spending while preserving anonymity.

Fungibility: is the property of a good or a commodity whose individual units are interchangeable. For example, one kilo of pure gold is equivalent to any other kilo of pure gold, whether in the form of coins or in other states, gold is fungible. Other fungible examples include, crude oil, shares, bonds, currencies. A diamond is not, since each is unique.

EOS: allows developers to create blockchain applications. Scalable and programmable, EOS has been called 'Ethereum on Steroids'. The EOS blockchain eliminates transaction fees and has the ability to process millions of transactions a second.

Casper + Sharding: the significant change coming to Ethereum over the next years is the proposal to switch from Proof-of-Work to Proof- of-Stake (as part of Casper), and break up the network into a bunch of partitions called shards. Each shard would have an independent state and transaction history. Validators on the network wouldn't be responsible for handling all transactions; instead, notaries within each shard would be responsible for their own shard.

Ethereum Viper: is a project created by Ethereum. It is an experimental programming language. It is an alternative way to build projects for the Ethereum ecosystem in the future. For now, coding with Solidity remains the primary programming language for the ecosystem.

MakerDAO: is one of the most prominent Decentralized Autonomous Organizations (DAOs) built on the Ethereum blockchain. One of their core products is the DAI stablecoin, which is a crypto-collateralized stablecoin.

Quantum Computing: as of 2018, the development of actual quantum computers is still in its infancy. Large-scale quantum computers would theoretically be able to solve certain problems significantly faster than regular computers. A quantum computer could efficiently break many of the security systems in use today. These systems are used to protect encrypted emails, secure web pages, and many other types of data. Breaking these would have significant consequences for electronic security.

Hashing: when a user sends a secure message, a hash of the intended message is generated and encrypted, and is sent along with the message. When the message is received, the receiver decrypts the hash as well as the message. Then, the receiver creates another hash from the message. If the two hashes are identical when compared, then a secure transmission has occurred. This hashing process ensures that the message is not altered by an unauthorized end user.

Quorum Blockchain: developed by J.P. Morgan, Quorum is one of the first major steps towards common adoption of blockchain among financial industries. Quorum is a permissioned blockchain infrastructure specifically designed for financial use cases.

Cardano Blockchain: similar to Ethereum, Cardano is a smart contract platform however, Cardano offers more scalability.

Dapps: Decentralized Apps. Dapps work in synergy with smart contracts and perform the role of an automated middleman. In the world of contracts when an agreement is reached, the broker ensures that the terms of the agreement are honored. A Dapp performs the same function using the blockchain to replace the broker.

DAUs: Daily Active Users

DADs: Daily Active Developers

Stablecoins: are cryptocurrencies that attempt to maintain a stable price; most attempt to peg their price to 1 US Dollar, but they could theoretically attempt a peg to anything, such as a basket of goods. A good number of people in the crypto community are skeptical that they will work.

Airdrops

Airdrop: airdrop is the process where a cryptocurrency team distributes cryptocurrency tokens to the wallets of some users for free. Airdrops are usually carried out by blockchain startups to boost their projects.

Reasons for an Airdrop:

To Reward Loyal Customers: blockchain services like cryptocurrency exchanges, trading platforms, wallet service providers, etc. wish to reward their customers and subscribers. This serves as an incentive that can help to keep clients loyal.

To Expand a Lead Database: airdrops can be used by blockchain firms to generate a valuable database of leads for their growing organizations. In exchange for free cryptocurrency tokens, users will be asked to complete online forms that contain valuable user information (email addresses) which can be used to develop marketing campaigns.

To Get the Word Out About a New Crypto: a new cryptocurrency can go completely unnoticed if it isn't given the right boost in terms of substantial marketing campaigns. With cryptocurrency enthusiasts looking for new cryptocurrency options, an airdrop is a way to get people interested in a new crypto.

Consensus Methods:

Proof-of-Work: is the first and most widely used method of establishing consensus. Proof-of-Work consensus is where each node is required to complete an extremely complex equation in order to finish each block.

The purpose of the complexity of the equation is to ensure that each node is forced to exert a significant amount of processing power and electricity in order to solve it. In return for solving the block, each node is given a block reward that typically comes in the form of cryptocurrency in addition to the transaction fees. This process is referred to as mining, and the nodes that choose to do it are called miners. In order to regulate this consensus system, if a miner gets a different answer than the other miners working on the same block, their answer is rejected. Miners don't want to use processing power and electricity without a reward, so they are economically incentivized to provide correct answers.

In a Proof-of-Work system, the only way to cheat is to control more than 51% of the ledgers, which is the same as possessing more than 51% of the total processing power dedicated to the platform. Even with this advantage, it would be extremely difficult to alter past transactions, and practically impossible to change transactions further than several blocks.

A miner that controls more than 51% of the processing power would have the ability to not only prevent transactions from executing and but also reverse transactions. This level of control would require a huge amount of capital (estimates are in the range of half a billion US Dollars), therefore it does not make much economic sense for a miner to attempt this kind of scheme.

The more processing power a miner has access to, the more likely it is that they will be able to correctly solve the solution to the complex equation first before other miners and win the block reward. A common practice has developed in which many miners join together and combine their processing power into a "mining pool." With this method, miners are usually able to generate a consistent income as opposed to sporadic and unpredictable income.

In mining terms, block difficulty refers to how difficult the equation for each block is to solve. If the blocks are being solved too slowly, then the block difficulty is reduced. If blocks are being solved too rapidly, the block difficulty is increased.

Good:

- Proof-of-Work consensus is capital intensive, and requires node operators to be heavily invested in the cryptocurrency that they are mining. This also functions as an economic measure against cheating.

- The potential profits that mining offers leads to the creation of more nodes, this has the effect of increasing the total computing power, improving the security of the network

The not so good:

- Proof-of-Work consensus uses a huge amount of energy. For comparison, one transaction using PoW consensus uses the similar amount of energy that an average household uses in a 24 hour period.

- PoW consensus typically has slower transaction confirmation times than other consensus methods

Examples of PoW Cryptocurrencies:

- Bitcoin

- Litecoin

- Bitcoin Cash

Proof-of-Stake (PoS): is a consensus method in which there are no miners. Instead, nodes are merely selected for the processing of transactions without needing to compute and solve complex equations. Other nodes in a Proof-of-Stake system will verify the block. In order to prevent cheating, nodes in a Proof-of-Stake system must lock a specific amount of currency in a virtual safe. This currency is forfeited as a penalty if any irregularities are detected. This process is known as Staking, and can be considered to function in a similar way as mining in Proof-of-Work systems but without the huge energy expenditure. The more currency that is staked by a node, the higher the chance that it will be selected to create the next block. This also means that nodes that attempt to cheat the system have more to lose in the process.

Good:

- PoS offers quicker confirmation times than PoW

- Proof-of-Stake executes more transactions per second than Proof-of-Work platforms

The not so good:

- There are remains a number of unanswered questions surrounding the security of Proof-of-Stake systems

Examples of PoS Cryptocurrencies:

- Peercoin

- Ethereum

Proof-of-Importance (PoI): users are obligated to provide as collateral a fixed amount of currency in order to become a node. The chances that they will be the node chosen to create a block and claim the fees depends on their importance score. The importance score of a node in PoI is determined by how frequently they use and add to the network. Nodes that send a huge amount of currency are often ranked with the highest importance scores.

Good:

- Proof-of-Importance consensus encourages the use of a cryptocurrency as a currency

- PoI rewards users that are heavily invested in the currency

- The Proof-of-Importance method appears to be secure and efficient

- Easily scalable

The not so good:

- The complex method used to determine the importance score has the potential to turn away new investors

Examples of PoI Cryptocurrencies:

- NEM

Delegated Byzantine Fault Tolerance (dBFT): in Delegated Byzantine Fault Tolerance, nodes are established by delegated shareholders. In order for a node to be elected, they are required to stake some of their currency. In Delegated Byzantine Fault Tolerance nodes are weighted equally.

A minimum amount of currency must be used as collateral for every node a user wishes to control. This makes it expensive to control more nodes, and more unlikely that any of these extra nodes will be elected. In dBFT consensus, shareholders are more likely to elect nodes that offer the lower transaction fees.

This democratic consensus technique both promotes usage of the network and lowers usage fees. The low transaction fees generated by dBFT reduces the overall profit profile offered by becoming a node, preventing potential abusers from achieving massive profits by establishing node pools. There is no mining in the Delegated Byzantine Fault Tolerance method. Financial benefits are provided in the form of transaction fees paid to nodes.

Good:

- Very quick confirmation times

- dBFT offers high transaction per second capacity

- Very low transaction fees– dBFT is currently transaction fee free

The not so good:

- The dBFT technique has not been tested at a large scale

Examples of dBFT Cryptocurrencies:

- NEO

Tangle: is technically not a blockchain. The Tangle consensus method utilizes a system that relies on every user of the network functioning as a node. Before a user can confirm a transaction, the user is required to validate two or more other transactions.

After the user has validated two previous transactions, a second user will validate the first transaction as part of their own transaction process. In this sense, the Tangle consensus method is closer to a net of transactions, in comparison to a blockchain with its chain of blocks.

The structure of Tangle provides users with free and instant transactions, and this scales well. There remains several questions regarding security and there is the issue that the entire network still requires super-nodes that moderate and oversee the network.

Good:

- Instant transactions

- Free transactions

- The low computational power demands by Tangle consensus makes it adequate for devices with low processing capacity, such as smartphones

The not so good:

- Tangle currently appears to be less secure than other consensus methods

- The Tangle network uses a Coordinator, which can be considered to function like a supervisor that guides the network until it is large enough to function autonomously. There is uncertainty regarding how efficiently the Tangle network will operate once the Coordinator is disabled.

Examples of Tangle Cryptocurrencies:

- IOTA

CONCLUSION

Thank you for making it through to the end of *Blockchain: Real-World Applications And Understanding.* Let's hope it was informative and that the pages were able to provide you with the knowledge needed to achieve the goal of expanding your understanding of blockchains. The next step, as I always recommend in my books is to take action by reading more or even taking one of my courses.

My others books that have been proven to assist professionals and investors are: *Technical Analysis for Forex Explained* and *Expert Advisor Programming for Beginners: Maximum MT4 Forex Profit Strategies.*

PROFILE OF
THE AUTHOR

Wayne Walker is the director of a global capital markets education and consulting firm (gcmsonline.info). He has several years experience in leading and coaching teams of Investment Advisors and has managed top performing teams in the Private Client Group based on Bench Mark Earnings (BME).